A Collection of Delightful Stories for Children

(Based on Islamic thought)

Author	:	Arif Mahmud Kisana
Translator and Editor	:	Muniza Tariq

★★

A Collection of Delightful Stories for Children
(Based on Islamic thought)

Author	:	Arif Mahmud Kisana
Translator and Editor	:	Muniza Tariq
Proofreading	:	Naveed Tariq
Composing	:	Sheraz Akhtar
Cover Design	:	Shehzad Ansari
Published	:	February 2017
Published by	:	Kisana Books Sweden
		Trollvägen 20
		19163 Sollentuna
		SWEDEN
Email	:	arifkisana@gmail.com
website	:	www.afkaretaza.com
ISBN	:	978-91-639-3143-7

This book is available at www.amazon.com

★★★

★★

5

DEDICATION

To all the children who motivated me into writing this book

★★★

★★

ACKNOWLEDGEMENTS

The original book was published in Urdu under the title *Sabaq Amoz Kahanian* by National Book Foundation Islamabad, Pakistan. The same book was Published by Amazon tilted *Dilchasp aur Anokhi Kahanian.*

After publishing of these stories there was a burning desire to have this work translated into English so that the children who can't read Urdu could understand these Stories. It was fortunate that Mrs. Muniza Tariq voluntarily took this solemn responsibility and completed this project in the shortest possible time. I can truly say that the completion of the English translation of the Urdu book presented a great challenge and it was possible only with the hard work and commitment of Mrs. Muniza Tariq. I do hope the children will find this book interesting and helpful in giving clear answers to their questions regarding Islam.

★★

8

★ ★

INTRODUCTION

Dear Children, This book is in response to all the questions that you have in your minds about the practical side of Islam. I've tried to address your queries in a simple yet interesting way that I hope will enable you to not only understand Islam but also enjoy reading about it.

It's natural for children to be curious about their religion and to know why they are expected to follow a certain faith. The questions might be simple but the answers sometimes are not and it's the responsibility of the elders to satisfy the curiosity of the children in a way that leaves no ambiguity in their minds about the integrity of their faith.

The aim and purpose of writing this book is to guide the youth in general and Muslim youth in particular, in a way that they become true, patriotic and respectable citizens of the world.

It is hoped that this book will be a valuable addition to the literature for children and that they'll be able to take guidance from it. It is also hoped that this book will provide basic information about Islam to children who may have certain doubts and vagueness about the faith they are following and are able to accept Islam with total sincerity and without any pressure.

★★★

I would like to thank His Excellency Muhammad Tariq Zameer (Pakistan's Ambassador to Sweden and Finland) who gave me invaluable advice in the publication of this book.

I would also like to thank Mr. Sharif Baqa (President, Majlis-e-Iqbal, London), Mr. Nasr Malik (Editor, Urdu Humasr, Denmark), Mr. Shahzad Ansari (Sweden), Mr. Sheraz Akhtar (Norway), Mr. Owais Jafrey (Seattle, WA, USA) and all the others who helped me in the publication of this book. I would specially like to thank my only sister Mrs. Tamsila Mutahir who encouraged me to write this book. Above all thanks goes to all the children who motivated me into writing this book.

Special thanks to Mrs. Muniza Tariq for the translation of Urdu book into English. I can truly say that the completion of the translation of the Urdu book presented a great challenge and it was possible only with the hard work and commitment of Mrs. Muniza Tariq.

Dear Children, Please give me your feedback about this book and if there's anything else you want me to write about then please do not hesitate to write to me so that in my next publication I keep that in mind. You can contact me via email arifkisana@gmail.com

Arif Mahmud Kisana
Stockholm, Sweden

****

PREFACE

Ever since the Universe was created man has been interested in telling and listening to tales. Even Allah has narrated stories in His scriptures about various prophets with a view to guiding humanity to the right path. Keeping this view in mind Mr. Arif Kisana has also written some stories for children so that their lives can take the right direction.

In order to make a story with a moral interesting, it's important that the plot of the story be so engaging and captivating that it attracts the attention of the reader but at the same time has a simple narrative style making it easy and understandable. Mr. Kisana has succeeded to incorporate both qualities in his writing.

Unfortunately, most Islamic scholars these days are not writing enough books for our youth living in the West. If we want our youth to stay in touch with our literary traditions then we'll have to make concerted efforts to establish this connection so that they can be beacons of light for the future generations. It's gratifying to see Mr. Kisana coming up with a book specifically designed to counsel our youth along Islamic lines. The stories are short and interesting and it is hoped that they will serve the purpose for which they have been written.

Muhammad Sharif Baqa
President Majlis e Iqbal, London

★★

FOREWORD

Creating stories for children is a challenging feat because the author must not only keep the perspective of children in mind but also make the stories interesting and informative. It's a challenge because in the modern age books have to compete with internet that offers a far greater range of entertainment and distraction.

One can feel a need for high quality yet fascinating literature for children living in the West so that they are able to comprehend the meaning of their existence in a way that doesn't seem to be forced. Mr. Kisana, who has been living in Sweden for over 20 years, has sensed this need and has created some very engaging stories with the idea of making the Muslim youth familiar with the Islamic traditions.

I hope Mr. Kisana's creation will be the catalyst in binding our youth with our Islamic heritage.

Tariq Zameer
Pakistan's ambassador to Sweden and Finland

★★

RELIGIOUS TRAINING AND COGNITIVE DEVELOPMENT OF CHILDREN

Our dilemma, while living in Europe, is that our children become disconnected with their Islamic heritage. What they are taught in schools often conflicts with what they are taught at homes and as a result of that there is confusion in their minds about what's right and what's wrong. They have questions to which there are no satisfactory answers. In situations like these sometimes even the parents are unable to fully explain the reasons for a certain belief that they are following.

Not just in Europe but also for parents living in Pakistan it's a cause for concern on how to bring up their children in a way that they can be a positive influence on the society they are living in.

We are fortunate that Mr. Kisana has been perceptive to this need and has written stories for children based on Islamic thought that will answer some, if not most, of the questions arising in their young and impressionable minds.

It's not easy to write ethical stories for children but Mr. Kisana has successfully managed to do so. The stories have been written in simple yet interesting style that is sure to get the reader's attention and to keep them involved.

★★

I hope the children will enjoy reading these stories and if they're too young to read then the parents will read them out for them. I also hope that the morals of these stories will be instrumental in making the readers a better Muslim.

Nasr Malik
Former Editor Urdu Service, Danish National broadcasting Corporation, Denmark

IMPORTANCE OF ISLAMIC EDUCATION AND MANNERS FOR CHILDREN

Reading these engaging stories took me back to the golden age when Western Europe was intellectually backward and stagnant, while Islamic scholarship flourished in all directions encompassing literature, art, natural and rational sciences. During the early history of Islam, education reflected the belief that raising children on correct principles was an obligation for parents and society. Islam, from its very inception placed a high premium on education. Knowledge (*'ilm*) as attested by the first revelation, occupies a significant position in Islam. There are innumerable injunctions in the Holy Qur'an like "Allah will exalt those of you, who believe and those who have knowledge to high degrees" (58:11), "O my Lord! Increase me in knowledge" (20:114) and "As Allah has taught him, so let him write" (2:282). These and similar verses provide a forceful stimulus to believers to strive for education and learning.

The most commonly used Arabic word for education is *ta'leem*, which means to know, to perceive, to learn, and to seek awareness through teaching. ***Ta'leem*** has two other integrants. One is ***Tarbiyah,*** which means to increase, to grow, to rear. It implies a state of spiritual and ethical nurturing in accordance with the will of Allah. Lastly is ***Ta'deeb***, which means to be cultured, refined, and well mannered. This suggests a person's development of sound social behavior conditioned by a deeper understanding of the Islamic concept of human being. Education thus covers a balanced growth of a person in rational, spiritual and social dimensions.

The first educational institution, which a child attends, is parental care. Neurological research shows that the early years play a key role in child's brain's development. The bonds children form with their parents are their first learning experiences, which deeply affect their future cognitive, emotional, physical and social developments. Optimizing the early years of children's lives is the best investment parents can make to ensure their all-round future success.

★★

Education for children is a great challenge in countries where Muslim children are exposed to a culture basically different from the Islamic culture. To meet such a challenge parents are required to fulfill their responsibility of imparting religious education in doses proportionate to the ages of their offspring. Engaging and captivating stories written in simple language by Arif Mahmoud Kisana, a versatile and eminent writer, will not only arrest the attention of children but also provoke their curiosity and in turn they will learn more. I am certain it will be a refresher to parents also. It gives me immense pleasure to learn that these stories are being translated in other European languages. We hope that today's children, the leaders of tomorrow equipped with knowledge and wisdom will recapture the golden age for not only Europe but the world at large. May Allah Almighty reward the author for such a noble undertaking. Aameen!

M. Owais Jafrey
Seattle, WA. U.S.A.

★★

★★

ABOUT THE AUTHOR:

Arif Mahmud Kisana is a Stockholm based full-time medical researcher and a part-time journalist. He's been living in Sweden since 1995. He writes articles and blogs in various newspapers and journals. The topics range from Islamic History to Social Changes, from Science to the Philosophy of Iqbal.

Arif Kisana has also been actively representing the Pakistani and Kashmiri community in Scandinavia for the last two decades and is a member of Foreign Press Association, Sweden. He is also the founder of Stockholm Study Center that meets every month to discuss solutions to social problems in the light of the Qur'an and the Sunnah of Holly Prophet.

Medical research is his profession, writing on social issues his hobby and the study of Iqbal his passion.
His collection of articles and columns Afkaar-e-Taaza has already been published. A Collection of Delightful Stories for Children is his second publication. He is also planning to publish A Collection of Delightful Stories for Children II, soon. He's also working on Iqbal and Dag Hammarskjold (A comparative study?), Sada-e-Hurriyet (Kashmir and Kashmir Movement), The Land of the Midnight Sun (Sweden and Northern Europe) and Awaz-e-Arif (a collection of essays).

★★

CONTENTS

WHY ARE WE MUSLIM?

WHY ARE WE MUSLIM?

Dear children, you may know that London is the capital city of England and the biggest city of Europe. There are many interesting things to do and wonderful places to visit in London. In the heart of this fascinating city lives a sweet little girl called Alisha. Alisha lives with her mother, father and two sisters. All of them live happily together. Alisha is the eldest and goes to school while her younger sisters Areeba and Inaya are too young to go to school therefore they spend their days playing at home.

They live in a lovely house not very far from Alisha's school. Close to their house is a park where the children often go with their parents and have lots of fun on swings and slides.

It was one of such beautiful day in the park when Alisha turned to her mother and asked, "Mama, why are we Muslim?" Her mom paused for a while and then said,' We were born in a Muslim family that's why we are Muslims."

Alisha thought about it for a while and then asked, 'So who is a Muslim and how are Muslims different from non-Muslims?"

Alisha's mom smiled and explained," The whole universe is created by Allah ... .this beautiful earth, this brilliant blue sky, the green seas, high mountains, deep oceans, lush green valleys, the sun, the moon and the stars ... everything. Allah has also created human beings and He has given some guidelines to us human beings and we are expected to live our lives according to those guidelines. This set of rules or guidelines is known as Islam. Those who follow these rules are called Muslims and those who don't are not Muslims."

Alisha thought for a while and then asked," How do we know about these rules?"

"All these rules or laws are explained to us in the Holy Qur'an," said Alisha's mom.

Areeba, who until now was listening quietly to her mom and sister, got interested in the conversation and urged her mother to tell her more about these 'laws'. Their mom explained that these laws were made to protect or safeguard the interests of the people and people were required to abide by those laws.

"Remember a few days ago we witnessed an accident where two cars crashed into one another?" Mom asked.

"Of course, I do. One was a red car and the other blue." Added Alisha. She remembered the incident clearly because it was the first time she had seen a collision between two cars.

"Yes, the same. Thank God that nobody was seriously hurt. Do you also remember that shortly after the accident the police arrived and they fined the man who was driving the red car because he had broken the traffic law by driving on the wrong side of the road?" Asked mom.

★★

"Yes, I remember and the driver of the blue car was not fined because he was following the traffic rules and driving on his side of the road," said Alisha.

"That's right. So you see just as people have made laws about how to drive safely so that there are no accidents, Allah has also made certain laws so that no human being gets hurt. If everybody follows those laws then there would be no accidents and nobody would get hurt."

'Can you give me an example of Allah's laws?" asked Alisha.

"Of course. Remember a few days ago your cousin Nasir burnt his hand because he was playing with the candle flame. Now it is a law made by Allah that fire will burn so if one will put one's hand in fire then one will end up burning or hurting oneself."

"So Nasir got punished for breaking the law of Allah by putting his hand on the candle?"

"Yes, despite his father's warnings not to do so." Explained Alisha's mom.

"Similarly there are other laws made by Allah and whoever will follow them will be safe and those who will not would be either hurting themselves or others. Following these set of rules is in fact Islam because Islam means obedience ... ..obedience of the laws of Allah."

"Are all of these laws given in the Holy Qur'an?" Asked Alisha.

"Yes, they are all explained in the Holy Qur'an that's why we should all read the Holy Qur'an to learn about these laws and to follow them so that we don't hurt ourselves or others." Said Alisha's mom.

It was getting dark now and Inaya was tired and getting restless so they all decided to go home.

Alisha gave her mother a big hug and said, "Thank you mom for explaining who a Muslim is and I promise that I will read the Holy Qur'an to know all about these laws and try to be a good Muslim so that I don't hurt myself or others."

★★

WHAT IS FAITH?

WHAT IS FAITH?

One day Alisha's father was sitting home and sipping tea when Alisha's mom rushed into the room in panic and said," Can you please go and fetch Alisha from school as I just got a call from the school saying she has a severe stomach ache."

Alisha's dad immediately got up forgetting his tea and picked up the car keys.

"On the way back can you, please also take her to the doctor?" asked Alisha's mom.
'Of course. Don't worry," assured Alisha's dad.

In school, Alisha's dad found Alisha doubled over in pain and crying. The school nurse was trying to soothe her. He immediately picked her up and took her to the doctor.

The doctor examined Alisha and asked her the usual questions about what she had eaten etc. and prescribed her some medicines.

Alisha asked the doctor if she'll be feeling better by the evening if she took the medicines.

'Of course, you will be fine if you take the medicine according to my instructions ... .one now and the other after 4 hours," assured the doctor.

★★

By evening Alisha was indeed feeling much better after just two doses of the medicine taken as per the doctor's instructions.

"Dad, the doctor is really good as I'm feeling much better now ...the medicines he gave me have worked their magic on me. Isn't it wonderful that we have doctors and there are medicines that take can make the pain go away. Can I go to school tomorrow?"

Alisha's dad said that she could if the pain didn't come back again.

"Dad, if I hadn't taken the medicine that the doctor asked me to, and in the way that he told me to, would I still be in pain?"

"Yes, whenever somebody is in pain or has an illness he/she must go to a doctor and then follow the doctor's instructions and take any medicines that are necessary. This is also a rule, we believe that doing certain things in a certain way will stop the pain or cure the illness. People have discovered these things by the knowledge Allah has given to them and we have faith in this knowledge," explained Alisha's dad.

"Faith? What's that?" asked Alisha.

"There you go again! You ask too many questions," ... teased Alisha's father. "But I appreciate that because asking questions is a sign of intelligence and one can learn a lot of things by being curious about them."

★★

"Let me illustrate what Faith is by giving you an example. Imagine someone who hasn't had anything to eat in days...he's extremely hungry and weak and … suddenly someone offers him his favorite dish...what will he do?"

"He'll devour it!" said Alisha.

"But before he has even taken a bite of it, the cook comes rushing in and tells him that he had accidently put poison in the dish instead of salt. Would he still eat it?" asked Alisha's dad.

"No, he will not because if he does he'll die," said Alisha.

"Exactly! No person, no matter how hungry he is, will never eat food that has been poisoned because he believes that if he does he'll surely die. Similarly it's our 'belief' that if we break the laws of nature or the rules made by Allah we'll be in loss. This belief in the laws of Allah is called Faith and whosoever believes in them and acts according to them is called a Momin. A Momin never harms himself or others because he follows the rules made by Allah."

"So it's important to have Faith?" asked Alisha.

★★★

"Absolutely! Believing in Allah's laws and following them means not harming ourselves or others. People, whether Muslims or not, should feel safe and secure in the company of a Momin. A Momin or a follower of Allah's laws is a source of blessing and happiness for others. Believing in Allah's laws is the basis of Faith. Just as we have faith that medicines will relieve us of our pain, we should have faith that following Allah's laws will bring us safety and happiness. It is so important that Allah calls Himself Al Momin ... granter of security."

"That means we should believe in the laws of Allah and follow them so that we don't harm ourselves and others?" asked Alisha.

"Exactly! It means that you've understood what Faith is. I know you're an intelligent girl. Now I can see you're feeling drowsy...it must be the medicines. I can tell you more about Faith some other day but right now you need some rest and sleep if you don't want to miss school tomorrow."

"Thank you dad for picking me up from school today and taking me to the doctor." said Alisha yawning.

Alisha's dad gave her a kiss and tucked her in bed and Alisha slowly drifted off a deep and peaceful sleep.

★★★

DIFFERENCE BETWEEN HUMAN LAWS AND THE LAWS OF NATURE

★★

DIFFERENCE BETWEEN HUMAN LAWS AND THE LAWS OF NATURE

"Mom, I'm very hungry...please give me something to eat!" shouted Alisha when she came back from school.

"You're supposed to say Assalamu Alaikum first when you enter the house, you should then wash your hands and face and then politely ask for something to eat,'" said her mom.

"I'm sorry mom but I'm so hungry today that I forgot to greet you. Can you please fix me a sandwich while I wash my hands and face?" requested Alisha.

"I've made some vegetable rice for you, you can have that if you're very hungry because making a sandwich will take some time."

Alisha was so hungry, she didn't protest in fact she enjoyed the rice so much that she thanked her mother for making them and also thanked Allah for giving them such delicious food to eat.

Feeling satisfied Alisha said "Mom, I told my friends what you told me the other day in the park and one of my friends Laiba wants to know if only those who are born in a Muslim family can be Muslims and those who are not can never be Muslim?"

"Laiba has asked a very sensible question. It's not necessary for one to be born in a Muslim family to be a Muslim but anybody who reads the Qur'an and accepts what's written in it and is willing to follow it can be a Muslim." explained Alisha's mom.

"The other day you also talked about the laws made by people and the laws made by Allah. If they are all laws then what's the difference between them ... . I mean how are man-made laws different from the laws of nature?" asked Alisha.

"You remember I gave you two examples to explain that...one of the accident of two cars and the other of Nasir burning his hand ... well in the first example if the police officer hadn't been there the driver of the red car after hitting the blue car could have simple driven off thus avoiding the traffic fine (punishment) but in the second example Nasir would have burnt his hand whether somebody was watching him or not. In other words Nasir would have been 'punished' for breaking Allah's law even if he were alone ... .so if you break a law made by people then there is a possibility that you can avoid being punished for it but that is not the case with Allah's laws ... .if you break Allah's law you will be punished for it .This is the difference between Allah's laws and the laws made by people," Explained Alisha's mom.

"There are two other differences between them," continued Alisha's mom." One can make changes in the laws made by people but the laws of Allah can never be changed."

"Really? How and why is that?" asked Alisha?

"People make and change their laws according to the changing needs of the people and times, for example in Sweden and some other countries the cars were used to be driven on the left hand side of the road but then this rule was changed and people now drive on the right hand side of the road. Governments often make new rules and make changes in the existing ones in order to suit the changing needs of the people and times. However, the laws of nature never change … they remain the same and it's not possible to alter them. Fire will burn everything that's put into it because Allah has given this quality to fire...it burned things a thousand years ago and it will burn things a thousand years later too. This is the nature of fire and it cannot be changed."

"I see ... and what's the other difference?" asked Alisha.

"The other difference is that man-made laws are or can be different in different places, for example in Sweden, Germany, Italy and China the law is for people to drive cars on the right hand side of the road whereas in England, Japan, Pakistan and Australia the law requires people to drive their cars on the left hand side of the road. There are other man made laws that are not the same for everybody everywhere."

"That's interesting ... but are the laws of Allah the same for everybody everywhere?"

★★

"Oh yes they are. Fire will burn everybody anywhere and every time if one puts his/her hand into it. If a Pakistani person living in Sweden puts his hand in fire it will burn him. Similarly if an Italian person puts his hand in fire in England his hand will also get burnt ... .whether he's a Muslim or a non-Muslim, young or old, man or a woman ... the laws of nature apply to all, every time and equally, that's why we have to believe in the laws made by Allah and act on them. This in fact is Islam."

'This was so fascinating. Thank you for telling me all that. Now I'll tell Laiba and my other friends about it too ... I'm sure they'll find it very informative too," said Alisha.

"I hope so. Now go up to your room and do your homework. After that I'll give you your favourite ice cream for listening to me so patiently." smiled Alisha's mom.

★★

WHAT ARE THE THINGS WE MUST HAVE FAITH IN?

WHAT ARE THE THINGS WE MUST HAVE FAITH IN?

Tehreem, Shahir and Maheen were very excited because their cousins Haris and Rukhsar from Pakistan were spending their summer vacation with them. Every day they would go out and explore something new. They had already visited the Wax Museum of Madame Tussauds, Buckingham Palace, Natural History Museum, The Big Ben and The Tower of London. Today the children's father was going to take them all to see the London Eye, also known as the Millennium Wheel, which is a giant Ferris wheel on the south bank of River Thames in London.

Haris had never been on a Ferris wheel before so he asked his uncle," Why is this wheel called London Eye?"

"It is called the London Eye because when the wheel goes up one can have a view of all of London. Just like one sees with one's own eyes one can see London through with this 'eye'."

"Isn't it scary ... .what if one falls down from the wheel?" Haris sounded a bit scared.

His uncle laughed and assured him that the capsule in which one sits is very safe and closed from all sides. It moves very slowly so that one can have a really good view while going up.

Haris now became very enthusiastic about the ride on the London Eye.

★★

They all took the London underground train to London
Eye. Haris and Rukhsar were amazed to see such a big
Ferris wheel and a bit afraid too of getting on it but once
they were on it they felt safe.
The view of London city from the London Eye was
breathtaking!

After spending a day along River Thames, the children
were all very tired and they just wanted to go home and
chat with one another. Once home, Tehreem's dad also sat
down with the children. Tehreem told their cousins that
their dad had told them some interesting things about Islam
so both Haris and Rukhsar asked their uncle to tell them
something interesting too.

"I promised Tehreem, Shahir and Maheen that I'll tell them
about the things that a Muslim must have faith in so if
you're interested and not too tired, I can tell you about
them now."

"Oh yes uncle please tell us about them." urged Haris.

"As you already know that faith is something that you
believe in with all your heart ... there's no doubt in your
mind about the truth of it. In Islam there are five things on
which we must have faith in otherwise we can't be
Muslims."

"What are those five things, uncle?" asked Rukhsar.

★★★

"The first and foremost is Tawheed ... believing in one God;Allah, the second is to believe in the messengers of Allah, the third is to believe in the divine scriptures (holy books), the fourth is to believe in angels and the fifth is to believe in the Hereafter. These five elements are also called the Articles of Faith."

" Does one have to believe in all five of them in order to be a Muslim or can one still be a Muslim if one doesn't believe in one or two of them?" asked Rukhsar.

"Just as you need a password to access your email or FaceBook account and if even one letter or digit of your password is missing or incorrect your account will not open just so you need to believe in all five of them in order to be a Muslim. If you don't believe in even one of them you won't be a Muslim." Explained Rukhsar's uncle.

"So in a way believing in all five of them is like having a password that will allow you to enter Islam?" asked Haris.

"That's right...you're a very clever boy, Haris."

"Dad, you said believing in one God is called Tawheed ... what does that imply?" asked Shahir who uptill now had been sitting very quietly.

"Believing in one God implies that we only pray to Him and nobody else. We only do things that will please Him. Having a firm belief that there is only Allah who controls everything is what Tawheed is."

★★

"And what is meant by believing in the messengers of Allah?" asked Maheen who didn't want to be left out of the discussion.

"Because Allah doesn't communicate directly with people, He appoints certain people who convey His message to everybody else. The people that Allah chooses to convey His message are called Rasool or His messengers like our Prophet Muhammad, Ibrahim, Jesus and Moses. A Muslim must believe that whatever these Rasools tell us is actually from Allah Himself and we must believe in them and follow them."

Shahir, who was all attention, said: "So, there are four messengers and they are Muhammad, Ibrahim, Moosa, and Eesa (Peace be upon all of them.)

Thanks for asking such an interesting question. In fact as our beloved Prophet Muhammad (PBUH) told us, Allah had sent one thousand and twenty four thousand messengers for the guidance of mankind and all were Muslims and they all taught Islam. Names of 25 of the prominent messengers are mentioned in the Holy Qur'an. Messengers who received revelations called messengers, whom I had mentioned earlier.

"And what are Divine Scriptures?" asked Tehreem.

★★★

"These are the Holy Books that Allah revealed to some of His Messengers like the Qur'an which was revealed to Prophet Muhammad (Peace be upon him) and Tawrat (Torah) to Musa (Moses), the Injil (Gospel), to Isa (Jesus), the Zubur (Psalms) to Prophet Dawud (David). The Holy Qur'an also mentions Suhuf-i-Ibrahim, scrolls revealed to Prophet Ibrahim. . The idea of these scriptures is to keep the religion safe from corruption and distortion so that after the death of the Messengers people can read them and take guidance from them. Everything that's written in them is actually Allah's words and we must believe in them."

As time passed, people made changes in the scriptures and the original messages of Allah were lost. It is only the Holy Qur'an, which is safe and Allah says in the Holy Qur'an that "He has revealed it and He will safeguard and protect it from changes."   All the copies of the Holy Qur'an written and published ever since it was revealed to Prophet Muhammad (Peace be upon him) centuries ago, and will be published until eternity will be identical and will never ever be changed."

"Why should we believe in angels when we can't see them?" Haris wanted to know.

"It's important to believe in angels because they carry out Allah's commands. We do not see them but they can see us."

"And what is the Hereafter?" asked Rukhsar.

★★★

"Akhirat or the Hereafter is the never ending or eternal life that will begin after our temporary stay in this one or in other words after we die. In the Hereafter, according to one's deeds in this world, Allah will decide who will go to heaven and who will go to hell. In other words Allah will reward those who have done good deeds in this world by sending them to heaven and punish those who didn't by putting them in hell."

"I don't want to go to hell," said Haris.

"Then you must be a good boy and don't ever_annoy me." Said his sister.

Everybody, including Haris's uncle and aunt enjoyed the comment and laughed.

Haris then asked "Uncle, you have explained to us very well. Please also tell us how we can define Islam in simple words?" Uncle replied: "Islam is an Arabic word derived from the word 'salaam'. This word encompasses (or covers) a variety of meaning like acceptance, obedience, peace, submission, and surrender. He continued: "Islam is a way of leading a righteous life as commanded by Allah in the Holy Qur'an and exemplified (or shown) by His last Messenger Muhammad (PBUH). "In other words, Islam is a Deen, or way of life, where one must have full faith in Allah's Tawheed and accept all His commands, faith that Muhammad (PBUH) is the last messenger of Allah and live life according to the instructions of the Holy Qur'an"

"Let me tell you an interesting fact Haris," added the uncle. "All religions of the world have been named after the name of their founders, or the name of the nation to which they were sent. For example Christianity takes its name from Jesus Christ, Buddhism form its founder Gautama Buddha, Zoroastrianism from its founder Zoroaster, Judaism the religion of Jews, from the name of the tribe Judah of the country Judea. But Islam enjoys a unique distinction as it doesn't convey any such relationship and does not belong to any particular person, nation, or country. It is not a product of human mind or limited to any particular people. It is a universal religion and its objective is to create in its followers the quality and attitude of Islam."

"Wonderful" exclaimed Haris. He thanked his uncle for all the good and useful information he had received and promised to always remember and follow it.

WHO ARE THE MESSENGERS OR MESSENGERS OF ALLAH?

★★

WHO ARE THE MESSENGERS OR MESSENGERS OF ALLAH?

"Ali, I'm going shopping, would you like to come with me?" asked Ali's mom.

"No, mom ... I have a history project to hand over tomorrow so I think it's better I stay home and work on it but can you please bring me a packet of potato chips?" asked Ali.

"Always eating junk food!" exclaimed Ali's mom.

"What is this History project that you're working on, Ali? Can I help you with it?" asked Ali's dad.

"We're studying about ancient human history ... how people in the old days lived etc. and I'm finding it very interesting." Said Ali.

"So what have you learned about it?" asked Ali's dad.

"So far we've learned that human history can be divided into four periods: the Stone Age, the Copper Age, the Bronze Age and the Iron Age ... .the age we're living in now. We've also learned that we can divide human history into three periods since the creation of the first man: the first period starts with Adam and ends with the birth of Jesus. The second period begins from there and lasts until a thousand years and the third period started about a thousand years ago till this day."

★★★

"That's wonderful ... you know so much already." Ali's father sounded impressed.

"That may be so but I want to know that since people lived differently in different ages so did Allah keep sending His messengers to them in the same way and also what was the need to send messengers ... couldn't people have lived without them?" Asked Ali.

"When Allah created man, He also needed to send His messengers from time to time so that the people could be guided to the truth and therefore live a pure life. The other reason for sending messengers was to give people the knowledge of Allah and His commands and how to act on them. All the messengers of Allah conveyed the message of Allah not only by telling about them verbally but also by acting on them. We have not been created to eat, drink and reproduce ... even animals do that ... the main purpose of our creation is to recognize Allah and give servitude to Him, so the main mission of the messengers was to tell people to worship one God and to live their lives according to His commands."

"So the messengers and messengers of Allah are the same thing?" asked Ali.

"Yes, they're both the same and it's important to know that whatever the messengers told people it was all from Allah. The messengers never told people anything that was not from Allah therefore it is important for people to do as the messengers said and did."

★★

"Did Allah send His messengers to people everywhere?" asked Ali.

"Yes, each prophet was sent to his particular people to remind them of the need to worship one God."

"How many messengers did Allah send on this earth?" asked Ali.

"We believe that Allah sent 124,000 messengers to mankind since the creation of man but Qur'an only mentions a few of them by their names like messenger Adam who was also the first man, messenger Nuh as in Noah's Ark, messenger Ibrahim, messenger Musa (Moses), messenger Daud (David), messenger Issa (Jesus) and messenger Muhammad.

"124,000 messengers! Wow ... that's a huge number of messengers. Why did Allah send so many messengers?" asked Ali.

"Allah sent a prophet to every group/tribe of people because after the death of a prophet there was a chance that the message of Allah would be distorted or changed ... .many unnecessary things added and necessary things taken out ... as in the beginning there were no reliable ways to record Allah's message except in people's memory therefore there was a need to keep sending messengers to remind people about the purpose of their creation. Also there was no communication between tribes in the old days as it is now so every tribe was sent a prophet so that they could understand the purpose of their existence."

★★

"Has there been more than one prophet at the same time?" asked Ali.

"Yes, there have been more than one prophet at the same time for example Messenger Shoaib, Messenger Musa and Messenger Haroon were messengers in the same period. Messenger Haroon and Messenger Musa were brothers."

"Very interesting … .and did they all preach the same thing? I mean were they all Muslim?" asked Ali.

"Yes, they were all Muslims and they all preached the same thing … that is to follow Allah's commands and to only worship Him."

"Is Allah even now sending his messengers?" Ali asked.

"No, Messenger Muhammad (peace be upon him) was the last messenger that Allah sent because he came at a time when people could reliably and flawlessly record Allah's message and communicate it with one another too. All the messages from Allah that Messenger Muhammad received through Angel Gabriel are recorded in the Qur'an. Many copies of the original Qur'an have been made and distributed to people everywhere. The Qur'an has been translated into many languages so that everyone can understand its message. Also everything that Allah wants people to do is given in the Qur'an so there is no need for any more messages from Allah."

★★

"If Messenger Muhammad is the last messenger of Allah then I should know more about him and the message that he gave but right now I must complete my history project. Also if my homework is not completed before mom comes she will not give me my potato chips." Smiled Ali mischievously."

"Next weekend when we have more time, I'll tell you about our beloved Prophet Muhammad (Peace be upon him)." Promised Ali's dad.

★★

OUR BELOVED
PROPHET
MUHAMMAD
(Peace Be Upon Him)

OUR BELOVED PROPHET MUHAMMAD

It was a weekend and as Ali's dad had promised he'll tell Ali about our beloved Messenger Muhammad (PBUH), so he asked Ali if he had done his homework and if he had the time.

"I've to go out with my friends for football but I do have some time before that so I think it's a good idea if you tell me something about Messenger Muhammad (PBUH) before my friends come to pick me up." said Ali.

"Yes, why not. As you already know that Messenger Muhammad (PBUH) was the last messenger of Allah therefore he's also known as the 'Seal of the Messengers'. He was named Ahmed at birth but his grandfather Messenger Abdul Mutalib, called him Muhammad. Actually both Ahmed and Muhammad have the same meaning and come from the Arabic word 'hamd' meaning praise. But we never call him just Ahmed or Muhammad because all Muslims believe that he is worthy of our deepest respect therefore whenever we mention his name, we say either Messenger Muhammad, Messenger Muhammad, Rasool Pak, Rasool-Allah or simply Huzoor and we always send peace on him and all the other messengers whenever we mention their names because all the messengers of Allah deserve reverence."

"When and where was Huzoor born?"

"He was born in 570 AD in Mecca, Saudi Arabia. His exact date of birth is not known but Muslims believe he was born

★★★

on a Monday on the 12th day of the 3rd Islamic month of Rabi ul Awal."

"Who were his parents?" asked Ali.

"His father's name was Abdullah and he died about two months before his son's birth. His mother's name was Aminah and she died when Huzoor was only six years old."

"Oh, that is so sad ... .so who brought him up after his mother's death?"

"His paternal grandfather, Abdul Muttalib...but when Huzoor was only eight years old, he also passed away and then his paternal uncle, Abu Talib took care of him."

So what was Huzoor's childhood like? Was he naughty like other kids?"

"No, he was not a naughty child. He never teased anybody or got into an argument or a fight with anybody ... and he never used foul language."

"Did he go to school?"

"No, he didn't go to school."

"Then what did he do all day?"

"Well he used to herd the sheep ... this was very common for young boys in Arabia at that time. Later when he was a bit older he started to do trade/commerce. He was very

★★★

well known for his honesty as a tradesman and people respected him for that. He never cheated anybody and he always kept his word ... .for that he was known as Sadiq (truthful) and Ameen (trustworthy)."

"Did Huzoor like children?" asked Ali.

"Oh he loved them! The children loved him too because he was always so gentle with them."

"So how did he find out that he was a messenger of Allah?"

"That's a very good question. He didn't know about it till he was forty years old. Ever since he was a young man Huzoor used to go to meditate in a small cave called Hira in a mountain near Mecca. One evening while he was meditating there, Angel Gabriel appeared to him and told him that. Angel Gabriel also told him that he should tell everyone that he was a messenger of Allah. Huzoor was asked to memorize whatever the angel told him and then he was to ask somebody to record/write it down because Huzoor himself couldn't read or write.This was the beginning of the revelation of the Qur'an."

"Wasn't Huzoor scared to see the angel and what did he do after that?"

"Yes, he was very scared so he came down and went home and told his wife, Messenger Khadija (Allah be pleased with her) about this experience."

"Did she believe him?"

"Absolutely! She had no doubt that her husband was a messenger of Allah and that he had received his first revelation."

"Who else did he tell?" asked Ali.

"He told his friends and relatives. His friend Messenger Abu Bakar Siddiq and a young man Messenger Ali and they both immediately became Muslims."

"Is he the same Ali after whom you've kept my name?"

"Yes, he's the one after whom we named you."

"Now I'm very happy that you've kept my name Muhammad Ali. They were both great men."

Ali's dad smiled and continued "Not everybody believed him though ... in fact a lot of people did not because he challenged the bad yet popular practices of the Meccans at that time and the Meccans did not like it ... specially the rich Meccans because Huzoor preached equality and justice. The Meccans of that time did not treat well and nicely the women, the slaves and the poor ... they had no rights and were at the mercy of their rich masters. Huzoor asked for their rights ... the Meccans felt threatened and as a result of that they started to make plans to kill Huzoor."

"Oh my God! What did Huzoor do then?"

"Well, he received a sign from Allah that he should leave Mecca and migrate to Medina which is about 400 kilometers from Mecca. So he did. This migration is known as Hijrat in the year 622 and that is the first year of the Islamic calendar."

"I hope the people of Madina treated him nicely?"

"Indeed they did. They were very hospitable and a lot of them converted to Islam very quickly. Hazoor's final resting place is in Medina too. He loved the city of Medina."

Just then the doorbell rang and Ali's mother announced that Ali's friends had come to pick him up.

"The timing couldn't have been more perfect ... thank you dad for telling me about Huzoor ... he was a great man! Exclaimed Ali and rushed out to greet his friends.

WHY IS ISLAM THE ONLY TRUE RELIGION?

WHY IS ISLAM THE ONLY TRUE RELIGION?

Maryam and Alia are very good friends and they often spend time together on weekends and during vacations. They also go together for Qur'an classes and exchange views on religion. One day Maryam came back to Alia's house after their Qur'an class because her father said he'll pick her up from there as he also had to pick up Maryam's younger brother from his football practice. Alia's father was helping Alia's mom in the kitchen but when the girls came, Alia's mom asked him to give the girls company.

Both Maryam and Alia were discussing their Qur'an lesson and Alia's dad joined in the discussion.

"Dad, how do we know that Islam is the only true religion because all religions preach good things and followers of all other religions think that their religion is the right one?

"You're right ... all religions teach good things like honesty, compassion, fairness, integrity etc. but what we need to ask is why do we need religion? A person can not understand everything about life by using his/her intellect alone ... people need guidance in life and this guidance comes from Allah through His messengers in the form of Wahi (revelation). Just as an eye needs light in order to see, our intellect needs guidance in order to live a pure life. Without this guidance people would take years to learn from their experiences but if something comes directly from Allah, only then we know that it's the right thing. Islam is the only religion that gives people this guidance ... not just on how to pray but also on how to behave in different social situations. In short Islam offers a complete code of life ... .a manual on how to live a moral life ... no other religion offers that."

'So Islam is more than just a religion?" asked Maryam.

"Indeed it is because it's not just about rituals ... all religions tell its followers that but Islam goes beyond rituals...it's a Deen meaning it gives us complete guidance on all the aspects of life from how to eat, sleep, walk, talk, dress etc. to how to conduct ourselves in our individual and collective life, in family and business, etc., ...no other religion offers that kind of in depth guidance because over the years all religions have been distorted and their original teachings have been mixed up as a result of human interference ... Islam is the only religion that is found in its pure form because Allah has promised to take care of the Qur'an Himself therefore whatever is written in the Qur'an is indeed Allah's word."

"Now I get the difference between Islam and other religions ... I used to wonder about it." Said Alia.

"So how should we behave with people of other religions?" asked Maryam.

★★★

"Islam teaches us to treat people of other religions with respect. Allah forbids Muslims from getting into arguments with people who don't believe in Islam. If they say something bad about Islam then you should just get up and leave and once the other person stops speaking badly about Islam then you should return. You may have noticed that during UN sessions if the ambassador of a certain country doesn't like or agree with what is being said about his/her country then he/she simply leaves the session showing his/her displeasure ... this is called "walk out". Similarly we should just "walk out' if we don't like what is being said about Islam."

"That is such a sensible thing to do." said Alia.

"Yes, Islam is a very sensible religion. Everything makes sense in Islam." said Alia's dad.

Just then Alia's mother brought some juice and sandwiches for them all and they all thanked her for that because they were indeed quite hungry.

★★

"Islam tells us even that Islam teaches us to treat people of other religions with respect. Allah forbids Muslims from getting into arguments with people who don't believe in Islam. If they say something bad about Islam then you should just get up and leave and once the other person stops speaking badly about Islam then you should return. You may have noticed that during UN sessions if the ambassador of a certain country doesn't like or agree with what is being said about his/her country then he/she simply leaves the session showing his/her displeasure ... this is called "walk out". Similarly we should just "walk out' if we don't like what is being said about Islam."

"That is such a sensible thing to do." said Alia.

"Yes, Islam is a very sensible religion. Everything makes sense in Islam." said Alia's dad.

Just then Alia's mother brought some juice and sandwiches for them all and they all thanked her for that because they were indeed quite hungry.

WHY ARE OUR PRAYERS SOMETIMES NOT ANSWERED?

WHY ARE OUR PRAYERS SOMETIMES NOT ANSWERED?

The Malik family was all sitting in front of the TV watching Pakistan Vs Australia cricket match. The atmosphere was charged because Pakistan needed only a few runs and it was the last over. Omar was loudly praying for Pakistan's victory whereas Saleh, Hussain and Laiba were praying in their hearts. Alas! Pakistan did not win the match. The Malik clan was very disappointed.

"I prayed so much for Pakistan to win the match then why did Allah not answer my prayers?" complained Omar.

"I prayed too." said Saleh.

"Me too." said Laiba.

"Well, not all of our prayers are always answered." said Omar's father, Mr. Malik.

"Why not? How come some of our prayers are answered while others are not?" asked Saleh.

"Let me explain to you why our prayers are sometimes not answered. Actually, the word to use here is not prayers but 'supplications'....when we supplicate we beg Allah for something only He can grant but there are certain conditions that a person must first fulfil before Allah can grant him/her wish. The first and the most important condition is to make every effort possible in accomplishing that task. For example, if you have an exam for which you haven't studied and then you pray to Allah that you somehow get an A then that's not going to happen so the first condition is to study hard and this is true for everybody whether they believe in Allah or not. Allah has made certain laws, and those who follow those laws are successful while others who don't ... no matter how much they pray ... are not."

"But dad Pakistani team trained hard for this match and all the Pakistanis prayed for them ... those living in Mecca and Medina also prayed for them and Allah doesn't reject the prayers of people in those holy places ... then why did they not win?" Asked Omar.

"May be the Australian team trained harder and longer for this match ... maybe they put in more effort and may be they prayed too. So success depends on a number and a combination of factors and not just prayers." explained Omar's dad.

"So what are those factors ... I mean what is the best way to ensure that Allah will answer our prayers?" asked Laiba.

"Like I explained before that if one follows the laws of Nature and puts in effort and hard work and then asks Allah for help only then Allah will answer one's prayers. Like in the Battle of Badr, which was the first battle between the Muslims and the Kuffar, (disbelievers) the Muslims under the guardianship of Messenger Muhammad (PBUH) made full preparations for the battle ... they trained hard and followed Huzoor's instructions and then prayed to Allah to give them victory over the non believers so Allah listened to their prayers and granted them victory."

"That means even the messengers of Allah had to pray and work hard?"

"Absolutely! All the messengers of Allah had to follow Allah's instructions and then prayed to Him to make them successful in their mission. When Allah told Messenger Nuh (AS) about the flood, Messenger Nuh prayed to Allah to save him and his people from this flood so Allah told him that He will save him and his followers from drowning if he built a big boat (ark) and hid in it ... so Messenger Nuh (AS) followed Allah's instructions and was saved from drowning. Similarly, Messenger Musa (AS) prayed to Allah to save his people from the arrogance of Firaun (Pharaoh Ramses II) so Allah told Messenger Musa to stay firm in the face of opposition from Pharaoh and He will grant him victory. Messenger Musa along with his brother Messenger Harun (AS) did as they were instructed by Allah and Allah ultimately gave them victory over the Pharaoh. So you see even the messengers had to work hard and follow Allah's commands and then pray in order to be victorious."

"If hard work is the key to success then what's the use of praying? There are many people in the world who don't pray but are still successful." asked Hussain.

★★★

"Well, Allah doesn't let anybody's hard work and effort go waste even if they are non-Muslims but if one prays along with hard work then things become very easy and success or achievement is guaranteed. Actually when Muslims supplicate they are asking Allah to guide them in the direction that's best for them and remember that when one supplicates to Allah after doing one's best then Allah doesn't disappoint him/her but the important thing is to do your best first. Another important thing to remember is that we should keep praying to Allah even if we think our prayers haven't been answered the first time because may be what we are asking for is not good for us. After praying to Allah we should just accept His will and not complain because only Allah knows what's best for us and we should just trust Him and His judgement."

"Now I know why I don't come first in my class." said Hussain.

"Because you don't pray?" asked Saleh.

"No, because I only pray and not work hard enough." said Hussain.

★★

★★

THINGS ALLAH HAS FORBIDDEN

THINGS ALLAH HAS FORBIDDEN

Isha didn't seem to be in a good mood when she returned home from school ... in fact she was so angry that she threw her bag on one side and ran up to her room without greeting her parents. Her mother asked her sister Hijab: "What was the matter with her and if both the sisters had had an argument."

"No, mom...it's not me but Maria. Both of them had a quarrel in school. I don't know what they were quarreling about because Isha was too upset to tell me," said Hijab.

"Okay, let me go up and ask her myself."

"Isha dear, get up and tell me what happened ... why are you so upset?" asked Isha's mom.

"I'm not getting up! I'm very angry because Maria pushed me and distorted my name and called me Isha Shisha. I'm not going to invite her to my birthday party and never going to speak to her again!"

"But why did she do that ... isn't she your friend?" asked Isha's mom.

But before Isha could reply Hijab said," It was Isha who started the whole thing because she refused to play with Maria and also made faces at her."

"It's because I was already playing with Khadija and Arifa and Maria was pestering me to play with her alone. I only

★★★

told her to go away and she got angry and pushed me and called me Isha Shisha. I'm always nice to her and never make fun of her big nose and dark complexion, like the other girls do, but she showed no regard for that."

"It's not good to make fun of people or to distort their names ... Allah doesn't like such actions." said Isha's mom.

"Does Allah get cross if we distort other people's names?" asked Hijab.

"Yes, Allah doesn't like insulting people and when you distort people's names it's like insulting them." explained Isha's mom.

"What else Allah doesn't like us to do?" asked Hijab.

"Not only that Allah doesn't like name calling, He doesn't like people who either criticize other people or blame them for doing something before first establishing the truth. Even if somebody has done something wrong one should not announce it to everybody . ... in fact one should try to hide his/her wrongdoings from others. We should also not be mean to others or make fun of their body parts or some other deformity that they may have. We should also not exaggerate something that someone has done or said or suspect them of thinking bad about you or form an opinion about them before first giving them a chance to prove themselves."

Both Isha and Hijab were listening intently to their mother because all this was new to them.

"We should speak gently to people and not raise our voice even if they are in the wrong. If we are having a discussion then we should listen to everybody's point of view with patience and try to counter their arguments with logic and not impose our views on them."

"What if somebody makes you angry?" asked Isha.

"Anger is one's worst enemy because when one is angry he/she can say or do something that he/she might regret later on."

"Then how should we deal with anger?" asked Isha.

"When one is angry, one should try to calm oneself down and remind himself/herself that Allah doesn't like it. Forgiving people for any wrong they have done to you is the best way to deal with anger. It's difficult to do so but not impossible. This is what Momins do. It's not advisable to act on one's anger and punish somebody for it ourselves because we don't have a right to do so. Only Allah can punish somebody for something. We should just focus on improving our own behaviour rather than picking up on other people's shortcomings."

"Maria also said that she wished my new watch which Dad brought me for my birthday either breaks or gets stolen...isn't that a mean thing to say?" asked Isha.

"Yes, it is and she shouldn't wish for that. This shows that she is jealous and that's not a good quality. If somebody has something nice then we should be happy for them and not wish for it to break or get lost. Also we should not talk behind somebody's back because Allah says talking behind somebody's back or in their absence is like eating the flesh of your dead brother. Allah also forbids us to find faults with others or to think less of them or be arrogant or proud of something that we have but others don't."

By now Isha's anger had subsided and she seemed more in control of herself.

"Tomorrow I'm going to apologise to Maria and ask her to be my friend again." Promised Isha.

"That's a good girl! Now come down and have a glass of milk." said Isha's mother.

★★

ETIQUETTES OF CONVERSATION

ETIQUETTES OF CONVERSATION

Saad and Samir were very excited because it was the last day of school before summer vacation and they were making plans about how they will spend their vacation.

"Let's ask dad to take us to uncle Zia's house in Sialkot," suggested Saad.

"Sialkot? No way! It's very hot in Sialkot in summer I'll ask dad to take us to Kashmir to uncle Tanvir's house. His house is in the mountains and there's a waterfall near his house too." Said Samir.

"But there's nothing much to do there other than going on walks ... it will be so boring!" said Saad.

"No, it won't be boring ... we can go on picnics ... we can go horseback riding ..."

But before Samir could finish Saad cut in. "No, I don't like horseback riding. I want to go to Sialkot so that I can play with Farhan and Farooq." shouted Saad.

Hearing the loud noises their father came in to check on them.

"Calm down boys! Why are you speaking so loudly?" asked father.

"We're making plans for our vacation and we can't agree on where to spend them." said Samir.

"There's no need to raise your voices ... that's bad manners." said father.

"But we're not fighting." said Samir.

"Even if you're not fighting or having an argument there are certain etiquettes of speech and we should be mindful of them." said their father.

"Really? What are the etiquettes of speech, Dad?" Saad asked.

"To begin with one should not raise one's voice while talking to others because speaking loudly may spark an argument."

"Even if one is angry can't one speak loudly?" asked Samir.

"Especially when one is angry because it can make matters worse. The other thing to keep in mind is to listen carefully to what the other person is saying and to not interrupt him/her mid-sentence. One should also talk sense and not argue for the sake of argument. If we do not agree with what the other person is saying then we should politely tell them so and then give our own point of view on the subject without getting worked up. It's also rude to make fun of people if they're having trouble with language or if they stutter.We should be patient with such people who have such shortcomings."

★★

"My friend Rehan stutters and it looks so funny." said Saad.

"It may look funny to you but imagine how he feels when you laugh at something he has no control over. It's not funny to him. We should always put ourselves in the other person's position and then see how it might feel and if you think people find your speech funny but you don't like them laughing at you then you should also refrain from laughing at others when they stutter."

"Nabil speaks wrong English and it's hilarious. We all enjoy it when he speaks English...he doesn't understand why we are smiling." Said Samir.

"That's bad manners too because it's like making fun of his speech."

"What else should we keep in mind when speaking?" asked Saad.

"The other thing that's important is to be careful of our choice of words ... we shouldn't use words that can hurt the other person and we certainly shouldn't curse or use foul language. Another thing that people don't pay attention to is that they'll report something malicious about someone without first verifying the truth of it. That is a sin! We should not spread malicious gossip even if it's true. We should refrain from hearsay because this is how rumours start. Exaggerating or playing down what someone has said in order to score a point is also wrong ... .we should always report the truth and avoid coloring it or mixing it with falsehood."

★★

"Our Islamiyat teacher was saying that we should be civil with one another when speaking. What does being civil mean?" asked Saad.

"Being civil means respecting one another and being civil in conversation means to speak to one another with respect and not being arrogant about our superiority over language or ideas.

"We should also not talk unnecessarily or be suspicious of other's intentions or try to see more into what they're saying. Similarly, we should speak very clearly so that the other person has no difficulty in understanding us. If one speaks plainly and openly then there are no misunderstandings."

"Did our beloved Messenger Muhammad (PBUH) observe all these rules of conversation?" Asked Samir.

"Absolutely! He had the best manners. Even in his speech he was observing what Allah had wanted for people to keep in mind when talking to others, therefore it's important for us to keep in mind all these things so that Allah is pleased with us."

"Now I'll try to keep all this in mind when talking to others and not make fun of Nabil when he stutters." Promised Saad.

"And I will not make fun of Rehan's English." Promised Samir.

★★

"You're both good boys and I'll take you to Kashmir for summer vacation and Sialkot for winter vacation. Is that a deal?"

"Yes!" exclaimed Saad and Samir.

★★★

ALL MUSLIMS ARE EQUAL

ALL MUSLIMS ARE EQUAL

"Why aren't we Chaudhry?" Ayesha asked her Dad as soon as she entered the house.

"What happened? Why are you asking me this?"

"My friend Faiza is very proud that she's a Chaudhry. She says Chaudhry is a superior caste. Is that right? Why aren't we Chaudhry? Can we change our caste and become Chaudhry too. What is caste?"

'Hold on! I'll explain it all to you," said Ayesha's father.

In the meantime Ayesha's younger sister Hajra and younger brother Qasim also came into the room.

"Caste is a system of social division based on certain common characteristics like in Pakistan we have the Chaudhrys, the Maliks, the Awans, the Rajas, the Qureshis etc. They share some common cultural features like language, beliefs and norms. No caste is superior or inferior to another. All human beings are equal in terms of their caste and they all deserve to be treated with respect. Allah has said that in the Qur'an that because we're all descendants of Adam ... no matter what our race or religion ... so we're all equal. No person is superior to another just because he/she was born in a certain family. These things are of no consequence in Islam. What matters, is person's moral deeds and his/her Taqwa, which is God consciousness ... believing that Allah has control over everything."

"But Faiza was saying that Qur'an talks about castes." said Ayesha.

"Yes, Qur'an talks about people being divided into nations and tribes but that is only so we can recognize one another. Qur'an also says that the only people who're superior to others are those who're more pious than others. Our Holy Messenger (PBUH) also said in his last sermon that Arabs do not have any superiority over non-Arabs, nor do the whites have any superiority over the blacks ... all men and women are created equal. He (PBUH) belonged to the tribe of Quresh, which was considered to be an influential tribe in Arabia in those days and he arranged a marriage of one of his cousins with Messenger Zaid who used to be a slave ... by doing so he proved to everybody that all were equal."

"If everybody is equal then why are people divided into different tribes and nations?" asked Hajra.

"That is for practical reasons only. It would be very confusing if everybody was a Khan or Khawaja...one wouldn't be able to tell which family the other was talking about. But this in no way means that the Khans are superior to Khawajas. Again what matters is one's piety. For example Shahrukh Khan or Amir Khan may be very popular and their fans may love them and admire them but if there's a non-Khan or somebody else, who doesn't belong to an influential caste, but is more pious than them

★★

then in the eyes of Allah he's better than Shahrukh Khan and Amir Khan."

"What is the difference between Shias and Sunnis because I've seen on Facebook that some people write they are Sunni Muslims and some write they are Shia Muslims? Are we Shia or Sunni" asked Qasim.

"I think you're spending too much time on Facebook Qasim! This division is not by Allah ...in Islam there's only one kind of Muslim ... one who fears Allah and follows His commands and He commands us to treat everybody equally and not to give anybody more importance because he/she belongs to a certain sect. In fact Allah sternly forbids people from doing that. Messenger Muhammad (PBUH) went so far as to say that those who create sects amongst Muslims are not one of us ... that means they're not Muslims. Therefore, we should only say we're Muslims and not Shia or Sunni. "

"Now if Faiza boasts about being a Chaudhry, I'm not going to be impressed and just ignore her." said Ayesha.

'And if somebody asks me if I'm Shia or Sunni then I will say I'm just Muslim." said Qasim.

★★

TREATMENT OF NON MUSLIMS

★★

TREATMENT OF NON MUSLIMS

Zohaib was very happy because his uncle, Mr. Tahir, was visiting them from Norway. Mr. Tahir had brought a lot of chocolates for Zohaib, which he had shared with his friends in school. Zohaib's friends also wanted to meet Mr. Tahir and to know something about Norway because they hadn't met anybody from Norway before, so it was decided that one day after school the boys will come to Zohaib's house to meet his uncle.

"Norway is not only one of the world's most beautiful countries, but it's also one of the most prosperous. Norway is a land of glorious glaciers and grand fjords. It has rocky coastal islands and many picturesque wooden villages. One can go for hiking, cycling and whitewater rafting in summer and dog-sledding, skiing and snowmobiling in winter." Said Mr. Tahir in excitement.

"What is the total population of Norway and how many Muslims are living there?" asked Sikander.

"The total population of Norway is about 5 million and out of this about 1.5 million are Muslims. There are about 30,000 Pakistanis and Islam is the second most practiced religion. In Norway's capital city Oslo there are many beautiful mosques where Muslims can go and pray whenever they want to. There are large congregations in these mosques for Friday and Eid prayers and other important Muslim festivals. Muslims are free to practice Islam. The State does not prevent them from doing so."

The boys were listening to Mr. Tahir very attentively.

"Do Muslims and non-Muslims get along well with one another?" asked Alim.

"Muslims and non-Muslims live in harmony...they treat one another with respect and tolerance. When it's Eid, our Norwegian friends greet us and similarly when it's Christmas we send them Christmas cards and if they are close friends then we also send them gifts."

'What does Islam say about relationship between Muslims and non-Muslims? Asked Naeem.

"Since Islam is a religion of mercy and justice therefore Muslims believe that it is not permissible under any circumstances for a Muslim to mistreat a non-Muslim. Muslims should not commit aggression against them or to frighten or terrorize them or to steal their wealth or deprive them of their rights. Muslims believe that it is obligatory upon them to honour agreements made with non-Muslim parties. If a Muslim has agreed to their conditions when seeking permission to enter their country (i.e., a visa) and has promised to adhere to that then it is not permissible for him to commit mischief in their land."

"What was our Messenger's behavior towards non-Muslims?" asked Zohaib.

"Our Messenger (PBUH) was very kind and just towards the non-Muslims. Once some Jewish men came to visit him

★★

in Madinah and when it was time for them to pray our Messenger (PBUH) allowed them to pray in Masjid-e-Nabvi in a Jewish manner. One day a funeral procession of a Jewish man passed in front of him, he stood up for it in respect setting an example of respect for the non-Muslims. Also the Messenger used to visit the non-Muslims who were sick."

"Can Muslims be friends with non-Muslims...is it allowed in Islam?" asked Alim.

"There are two kinds of non-Muslims...one kind is of those who are the enemies of Muslims and openly mistreat them and hate them ...obviously one can not be friends with them and the Qur'an also forbids us from associating ourselves with them. The other kind is of those who do not hate the Muslims and treat them fairly therefore it's perfectly acceptable to keep good and friendly relationships with them. There are many Muslims living in non-Muslim countries and many non-Muslims living in Muslim countries, how then is it possible for them to live peacefully if they don't respect one another's religious beliefs? As Muslims it's our religious duty to bring non-Muslims towards Islam and the best way of doing this is by being a good Muslim:...by not lying, not cheating, not stealing, not spreading aggression, and by being honest etc."

"Uncle, you said Islam allows religious freedom...what does that mean?" asked Naeem.

"This means that there is no compulsion in religion; one can choose whichever religion one wants to follow ... no one should force anybody to follow this or that religion. There is no punishment for somebody who doesn't follow Islam. The duty of our Messenger Muhammad (PBUH) was only to deliver the message of truth and no more. Islam forbids us to mutilate or destroy the places of worship of other religions like churches and synagogues ... even temples. In fact, if the need be these places of worship should be protected from destruction. Islam forbids us to speak ill of other religions and their gods."

"But what if a non-Muslim speaks ill of Islam...what should we do then?" Asked Sikander.

"The Qur'an says that if somebody is making fun of Islam or if somebody is speaking against Islam then the best thing to do is to leave such a place and return only when they have stopped talking badly about Islam."

"Uncle, I've heard that in Norway, in summer the sun never goes down and in winters it's mostly night...how does one deal with that?" asked Zohaib.

"Yes, it's very interesting. A quarter of Norway's territory lies north of the Arctic Circle and because of the rotation and the revolution of the earth the other Scandinavian countries like Sweden and Finland also experience long days in summer and very short days in winter. North Cape is considered to be the northernmost point in Europe and the sun doesn't set there from 14th May to 31st of July, therefore it is known as the Land of the Midnight Sun. But no matter how long or short the days are people in these regions go about their daily lives according to the time. In

★★★

summer people go to bed while it's still daylight outside and in winter people go to work and children go to school when it's still dark."

"Sounds strange but interesting. I would like to experience that someday." Said Sikandar.

"Well, you can if you study hard and come to Norway for higher studies...that way you can experience the interesting phenomenon of the Midnight Sun and also pursue a degree."

"Thank you uncle for telling us about how we should treat the non-Muslims, and also about Norway. Norway sounds like an interesting country and I hope to visit it someday." said Zohaib.

WHY CAN'T WE SEE ALLAH?

WHY CAN'T WE SEE ALLAH?

In a small town, but a big house in Pakistan, there lived a sweet little girl named Mashal who loved animals. She loved animals so much that her parents had made a small zoo in the backyard of their house where they kept small domesticated animals like dogs, cats, rabbits etc., and some birds like peacocks and parrots for her amusement. Mashal would go and check on them first thing after coming back from school. She was especially fascinated by the beautiful colours of the peacock and the parrots. She would play with her pets for hours. Inside the house there was also a small aquarium with brilliantly coloured small fishes.

One day Mashal asked her mother as to who had created such beautiful creatures.

"Just like Allah has created us He has created all the other creatures ... .not just the creatures but everything else in this world and beyond ... like the sun, the stars, the mountains, and the oceans ... the whole universe." Explained Mashal's Mom.

"If Allah created everything then who created Allah?" asked Mashal.

"Well, you've asked me the same thing that I used to wonder about when I was your age. It's difficult to explain this because you're still too young to understand this concept but I'll try to explain it to you in the best way possible."

★★

"So, you were also curious about it when you were younger?" asked Mashal.

"Everybody at some point in his/her life thinks about it ... it's natural for one to be curious about the origin of everything that we see and things that we don't see but know they are there. Allah is an existence that we can't see but can feel His presence in everything that we can see. He's not like us or anything else that He has created because there's no one and nothing like Him. He's the creator of everything and is therefore unique. He's present in everything and is everywhere. We recognise Allah by the signs in nature that point to the Creator and human instinct accepts the existence of the Creator through those signs."

"If Allah is present everywhere then why can't we see Him? Is it because He's very high up in the sky?" Mashal asked.

"No, it's not that Allah is sitting somewhere up in the sky but like I said before He's present everywhere. Just because we can't see Him doesn't mean he doesn't exist, but His existence can be 'felt' and not seen for example we cannot see air but we know it's there because we can feel it ...no living thing can live without it similarly we cannot see heat and cold but can 'feel' them. There are magnetic waves that we cannot see but know they are there. We can 'feel' pain but not see it and just because we cannot see pain we can't say it doesn't exist. A thing doesn't need to have physical form in order to exist. Allah doesn't have a physical form but He exists and we know that because we can feel His existence in the things He has created ... everything in this universe points to a Creator and that Creator is Allah."

"I don't understand how can one know of the existence of Allah through His creations?" asked Mashal.

"Well, in this universe there are trees, mountains, oceans, sun, moon, stars, animals, human beings etc. How did all of these come to be? Who made all of these things? Did they come to be on their own? No, it's not possible. Everything needs to be 'created' by someone or some force and that someone/force is Allah. If we observe the various signs in nature like the birth of human beings, the rotation of the earth and the stars, the clouds and the rain, the night and the day, different types of fruit and flowers, the big animals like the whales and microscopic organisms that we cannot even see...they all point to the existence of a Supreme Being, Who created them i.e., Allah. Nothing and nobody other than Allah has the power to make anything. One only has to look at how human beings are formed from a single cell, to a living, breathing, thinking person who is not aware of how his bodily functions are taking place even while he's sleeping. How the human brain processes information and stores it is also amazing and can only be possible if there's a Supreme force making it work that way. This universe is so vast that we cannot even imagine but everything in it is moving in a set pattern and direction without anything colliding with another. Night and day and seasons all come and go at a set time. Do you think there's nobody controlling it ... .we cannot control these things leave alone, make changes in them if we wanted to and this is what

★★★

Messenger Ibrahim (AS) tried to explain to the king who claimed to be god."

"Really? Who was Messenger Ibrahim (AS) and who was the king who claimed to be god?' Mashal was interested in knowing.

"Messenger Ibrahim (AS) was a Messenger of Allah a long time before Messenger Musa (AS). He lived in present day Iraq. He had two sons who were also messengers: Messenger Ismail (AS) and Messenger Ishaq (AS). His grandson Messenger Yaqoob (AS) was also a messenger. The Kaaba in Mecca was built by Messenger Ibrahim (AS). During his time people used to worship the sun, the moon and the stars and also the idols. He tried to tell them that how can something that has no will of its own or can speak or move can be god but people were not convinced. One day he went to the temple where all the statues were kept and shattered them all except the biggest one and kept his axe on his shoulder. When King Namrud and his people saw the broken statues they were very angry and asked Messenger Ibrahim (AS) if he had done it. He said to them to ask their biggest god who had done it. To this they replied that the god was made of stone and hence couldn't speak. Messenger Ibrahim had made his point and he said to them that if something could not move or speak then how could it give you profit or loss so what was the point of worshipping such a god?

When Namrud heard about it he asked for Messenger Ibrahim (AS) to be burned alive in a fire but by the grace and will of Allah Messenger Ibrahim (AS) was saved."

★★

"That is so interesting. Thank you for giving me such useful information. You have answered a lot of questions I had in my mind about the existence of Allah. I now know that even though we cannot see Allah He certainly exists."

★★

WHAT THE QUR'AN SAYS ABOUT ALLAH

WHAT THE QUR'AN SAYS ABOUT ALLAH

Mashal and her cousins Abdullah and Aira had just come back home after spending a fun filled day at Rawal Lake with their parents. They were a bit tired after paddle boating in the lake for two hours and now they just wanted to sit and chat. Mashal started to tell Abdullah and Aira about the discussion she had with her mother about Allah. Both Abdullah and Aira were interested in knowing about it because they were fascinated by the fact that one could 'feel' Allah's presence in everything even though He couldn't be seen. They hadn't thought about it this way before. Just then Mashal's mother walked in and Abdullah asked her to tell them more about Allah.

"What does the Qur'an say about believing in God?" asked Abdullah.

"The first thing we need to know is that the proper term to use for God is Allah because it's the personal name of the One true God. Nothing or no one else can be called Allah. The term has no plural or gender. This shows its uniqueness when compared with the word god, which can be made plural, gods, or feminine, goddess.

The Qur'an asks us to believe in one God i.e., Allah. Believing in one God means that we believe that He's the Supreme Being and is the creator and the sustainer of everything in this universe and things beyond this universe. He's unique, eternal and everlasting meaning there's nothing else is like Him; He always has been and always will be ... even when everything else will die or finish. The Holy Qur'an speaks of the existence of Allah... in fact the Qur'an is a proof of the existence of Allah because nobody else could've written such an amazing book. Actually, Qur'an is the connection between us and Allah. Qur'an tells us to believe in Allah and to surrender ourselves to His will and commands."

"What is meant by Allah's will and if everything happens with Allah's will, then what's the point of our struggle?" asked Mashal.

"This is a very good question and it can be explained in three stages. The first stage was when Allah created the universe and at that stage He created it the way He wanted it to be ... .He created the sun, the moon, the stars, and the earth etc. The second stage was when he created
the laws for the functioning of the universe . Everything in this universe functions according to those laws and nobody can make any changes in them. For example, He gave fire the property of heat and water the property of wetness and nobody can take these properties away from them. Then came the third stage in which He created human beings and made certain laws for them. The only difference between the laws of Nature and the laws of Man is that whereas nature has no will of its own other than that of Allah's, Man has been given free will i.e., Man can choose to be good or bad and he only can be responsible and accountable for his deeds. For example if you don't go to school and study and then fail the exams, you can't blame Allah for it and say that it was His will that I failed. This rule also applies to all the other aspects of our lives."

"If we have been given free will then how can we benefit from believing in one God in our practical lives?" asked Aira.

"Believing in one God doesn't only mean that we accept His existence but it also implies that in our daily lives we should only ask Him for help and when one believes that only Allah can help then one doesn't need the help of anybody else and that saves one from being corrupt and dishonest and from trying to please others ... it makes us God- reliant and Allah says that whoever relies on Him, He will not disappoint him/her."

"If Allah knows everything then does it mean He has eyes and ears by which He sees and listens to everything?" Abdullah asked.

"When we say that Allah sees and hears everything that doesn't mean that He sees with His eyes or hears with His ears but it means that He's aware of whatever is going on. He's not like His creatures because if He had eyes and ears He would be like His own creation."

"Does God only have one name, Allah?" asked Mashal.

★★

"Allah has described Himself in the Qur'an through various names. All of His names represent His attributes e.g., one of His names is Ar Rahman which means merciful, then there's Al Ghaffar meaning ever forgiving, Al Khaliq meaning the creator, Al Khabeer meaning all-knowing etc. There are 99 names of Allah and each of these beautiful names represents one of His beautiful qualities. Muslims believe that studying these names and attributes of Allah is one of the most effective ways of strengthening one's relationship with Allah."

"How can we know about the laws of Man?" asked Abdullah.

"All the laws of Man have been given in the Qur'an and our Messenger Muhammad (PBUH) practised those laws in his daily life and we should also try to act according to those laws so that Allah is pleased with us."

★★

WHO IS A MOMIN?

WHO IS A MOMIN?

"Where's Grandpa?" asked Shumail as soon as he came back from school.

"He must be resting in his room...why do you want to see him?" asked Shumail's mother.

"This is between him and me," replied Shumail and rushed towards his Grandpa's room.

Yawar and Anusha were curious to know what Shumail wanted with Grandpa so they also followed him into Grandpa's room.

"Assalamualaikum Grandpa."

"What brings you all to my room today?" Grandpa was surprised and asked.

"Actually, I wanted some information from you ... there's an essay writing competition in my school and I'm participating in it and I want you to help me understand the topic so that I can write a good essay." Explained Shumail.

"What is the topic of the essay?" asked Grandpa.

"The topic is Life of a Momin...can you tell me who a Momin is and what kind of life he leads?" asked Shumail.

★★★

"Sure..why not. Momin is an Arabic word meaning 'believer'. It refers to a person who submits himself completely to the will of Allah and has faith firmly established in his heart i.e., a committed and devoted Muslim."

"But you told us that a Muslim is a believer and he also submits himself to the will of Allah ... so what's the difference between a Muslim and a Momin?" asked Yawar.

"That's a very good question. The difference between a Muslim and a Momin is the difference in the level or degree of faith. They both accept Islam as a religion, they both believe in Angels and the Day of Judgement and they both follow the rituals of Islam like offering salat and fasting etc. but a Momin is one who has achieved a higher level of faith (iman). He's a true believer...he has grasped the real message of Islam and he puts his trust in Allah completely and without any reservations (tawakkul)."

"So it means that when somebody accepts Islam he/she becomes a Muslim and when he/she lives his/her life according to Islam he/she becomes a Momin? Asked Anusha.

'That's exactly right ... all Momins are Muslim but not all Muslims are Momin."

"What are the attributes of a Momin?" asked Shumail.

" A Momin is a believer who remains unshaken in adverse conditions because he believes that they are a test from

Allah and he has to remain steadfast. He doesn't complain about anything, in fact he shows gratitude to Allah even when he's going through hardships. He's patient and Allah fearing...he's chaste and pious...he praises Allah and above all he believes in the unseen i.e., Allah, and turns only to Allah for his salvation."

" Does a Momin never do anything bad or evil?" asked Yawar.

"Well Mumins are human beings too so they can sometimes do wrong things but as soon as they realise they've displeased Allah, they repent and ask Allah for forgiveness because they are not arrogant and know they can commit sins."

"Was our Messenger Muhammad (PBUH) a Momin too?" asked Anusha.

"He (PBUH) is the best example of a Momin because he (PBUH) did everything that Allah ordered him to. He (PBUH) never told lies, never cheated anybody, never hurt anybody, he was always patient and polite with people. He (PBUH) prayed regularly and gave charity and fearlessly spread the message of Islam despite threats to his life. That is the essence of a true believer; to stay firm in the face of adversity because of your complete and unshakable faith in Allah."

"Does that mean that all the other messengers of Allah were Momin too?" asked Yawar.

★★★

"Absolutely!"

"Can ordinary people like us become Momin too?" asked Shumail.

"No doubt becoming a Momin is difficult but not impossible. We can at least 'try' to be like a Momin and ask Allah to help us along the way ... that way even if we don't become a Momin we can at least become a better Muslim."

"I want to become a Momin." said Yawar.

Grandpa laughed and said ' For that you'll have to choose the same thing for others that you choose for yourself and not like the other day when you kept the good candy for yourself and the one you didn't like you saved for Anusha and Shumail."

"Really?" Asked Yawar surprised.

'Really! Our Messenger said that you cannot become a Momin till you like for others what you like for yourself. He also said that a Momin doesn't say or do things that can hurt others."

Yawar looked embarrassed but he promised that he would 'try' to be a Momin and not tease Shumail and Anusha and give them the same candy as he was having himself.

★★

★★

EXEMPLARY PERSONALITY

★ ★

EXEMPLARY PERSONALITY

Ibrahim was feeling very proud and excited because he had won his first ever inter - school speech competition. He wanted to share the good news with his family and specially his grandad who had helped him in writing his speech.

" Grandad, (Grandpa was used earlier; is good to be consistent) I got the first prize in the speech competition!" exclaimed Ibrahim.

"That's excellent. I was praying the whole day for you."

'Your prayers and your help in writing the speech helped me in winning this competition. Thank you very much! It was a tough competition and initially I was very nervous too but when I started speaking, the whole hall fell silent and when I finished everybody clapped. When the Chief Guest gave me the prize, he told me that I had spoken well on a Momin's life and that I should also try to inculcate the attributes of a Momin in my personality and if I do that I can be a role model for others." Said Ibrahim.

"That's a very good advice."

"Who's a role model and what kind of character does he have?" asked Ibrahim.

"A role model is someone who has an admirable character, has good manners and high morals. He's someone who sets an example of exceptional behaviour for others to follow."

★★

"Are there people in this world who can be role models for us?" asked Ibrahim.

'Yes, there are many but the best and the greatest role model for us is the Messenger Muhammad (PBUH). The Qur'an says that he's the ultimate example of a perfect personality."

"Wow! Can you tell me about our Messenger's character and what his companions thought of him?"

"Of course. Our Messenger (PBUH) was the epitome of good manners. He always treated children with kindness ... he enjoyed their company and played with them to make them happy. He had a fine sense of humour...it was not vulgar and it never mocked or debased anyone. He was a lover of peace and he wanted people to live in harmony and to settle their differences without resorting to violence. He used to greet people with Salaam/AssalaamuAlaikum first. He had a very pleasant personality and greeted people with a smile and spoke to them with gentleness.
He was very generous and always put other people's needs before his own. He was very caring of the rights of the women and commanded his followers to give special treatment to women by giving them respect and equal rights. He was very considerate towards the orphans and asked his companions to take special care of them. He was not only considerate towards people but also towards animals and told people to treat them with kindness because they were also a creation of Allah. He was a modest, generous and a selfless man."

★★

"What did he look like ... I mean what was his appearance like?"

"Well, he was of medium height...neither very short nor very tall. Similarly the colour of his skin was neither very light nor very dark but his face shone like that of a full moon. His hair was neither long nor short, not straight but not curly either. His eyes were black and eyebrows were long. He had a strong body which was neither flabby nor very thin. In short, he was beautiful and he exuded strength and confidence and people were in awe of his personality."

"So if I want to be a role model for others what kind of attributes should I have?" Ibrahim asked yet another question.

"Like I explained to you earlier that the most perfect personality is that of our Huzoor's so you should try to emulate him if you want to set a standard of good character and personality ... in other words you should be honest, sincere, truthful, modest, obedient, hardworking, punctual, efficient, polite and gentle towards everybody. You should not cheat others or be lazy. You shouldn't be jealous or envious of others or be argumentative. You shouldn't mock or make fun of others and not consider yourself superior to others especially now that you've won the first prize in the speech competition," smiled Ibrahim's grandad.

"But Grandpa it seems so difficult to do all that ... . It's almost impossible!"

★★★

"No, it isn't! It may seem difficult but it's possible. You can slowly and gradually give up your bad habits and at the same time you can start working on the good qualities. If one is determined to change oneself for the better then Allah also helps him/her along the way. It might take a long time ... sometimes one's whole life, but if you're conscious and bent upon improving yourself then improvement will take place and you can be an exemplary person that people will admire and respect."

'I'll try to be a good person that other people can trust and admire. I'll try to be like our Messenger Muhammad (PBUH) and give respect to others so that they give me respect in return." Promised Ibrahim.

"You're a good boy, Ibrahim and I have faith in you. I know you can be a role model for others if you don't give up trying to be a man of good character."

Just then Ibrahim's Mom and Dad entered the room surprising him with his favourite chocolate fudge cake to celebrate his success.

★★★